Raspberry PI 3:

The Ultimate Beginner's Guide

Lee Maxwell

© 2016

TABLE OF CONTENT

Introduction

I want to thank you and congratulate you for downloading the book, Raspberry PI 3: The Ultimate Beginner's Guide".

This book contains proven steps and strategies on Raspberry PI 3... The original Raspberry Pi chip worked at 700 MHz as a matter of course, and did not get to be distinctly sufficiently hot to require a warmth sink or extraordinary cooling unless the chip was overclocked. The Raspberry Pi 2 keeps running at 900 MHz as a matter of course; it likewise does not get to be distinctly sufficiently hot to require a heatsink or uncommon cooling, despite the fact that overclocking may warm up the SoC more than expected.

Most Raspberry Pi chips could be overclocked to 800 MHz, and some to 1000 MHz. There are reports the Raspberry Pi 2 can be also overclocked, in outrageous cases, even to 1500 MHz (disposing of all wellbeing highlights and over-voltage impediments). In the Raspbian Linux distro the overclocking alternatives on boot should be possible by a product charge running "sudo raspi-config" without voiding the guarantee. In those cases the Pi consequently close the overclocking down if the chip comes to 85 °C (185 °F), however it is conceivable to abrogate programmed over-voltage and overclocking settings (voiding the guarantee); a fittingly estimated heatsink is expected to shield the chip from genuine overheating.

More up to date forms of the firmware contain the alternative to pick between five overclock ("turbo") presets that when utilized, endeavor to boost the execution of the SoC without impeding the lifetime of the load up. This is finished by observing the center temperature of the chip, the CPU stack, and progressively changing clock speeds and the center voltage. At the point when the request is low on the CPU or it is running excessively hot the execution is throttled, yet in the event that the CPU has much to do and the chip's temperature is satisfactory, execution is briefly expanded with clock rates of up to 1 GHz contingent upon the individual load up and on which of the turbo settings is utilized.

Thanks again for downloading this book, I hope you enjoy it!

Chapter 1

Raspberry Pi 3

The Raspberry Pi 3's unpretentious enhancements indicate a noteworthy ease of use and execution update

Credit: Brad Chacos

More like this

-

Supercharged Raspberry Pi 3 includes Wi-Fi, Bluetooth, and more speed, yet at the same time...

-

10 shockingly down to earth Raspberry Pi ventures anyone can do

-

Smaller than normal PC intrusion: These fundamentally minor PCs fit in the palm of your hand

-

Video

Lenovo Yogabook Review: Innovative touch abilities caught in a something else...

-

51% off Apple USB-C to Lightning Cable - Deal Alert

-

17% off Wonder Workshop Dash Robot - Deal Alert

-

53% off Apple USB-C to USB Adapter - Deal Alert

At a Glance

• The Raspberry Pi Foundation Raspberry Pi 3 Model B

PCWorld Rating

The Raspberry Pi 3's inconspicuous upgrades include, supercharging execution considerably further and dispensing with what few waiting setup bothers stayed in the Raspberry Pi recipe, all while keeping up the...

My, what deluding looks like can be.

At first become flushed, the Raspberry Pi 3 Model B shows up physically indistinguishable to the year-old Raspberry Pi 2 Model B: a similar port choice, the same GPIO stick design, a similar essential board format, and whatnot. Be that as it may, don't let that trick you! The jump to the Raspberry Pi 3 is similarly as noteworthy as the earlier update, supercharging execution considerably further and taking out what few waiting setup bothers stayed in the Raspberry Pi recipe, all while keeping up a similar bargain basement $35 value point.

In any case, while the Raspberry Pi 3 is effortlessly the most advantageous and intense Raspberry Pi ever, and the primary that can conceivably be utilized as an appropriate PC, it's still a greater amount of a transformative update than a progressive one—which is really something to be thankful for, as it aides the RP3 keep up in reverse similarity with past eras of the cherished smaller than normal PC and producer board.

Official merchant Element 14 sent us a Raspberry Pi3 Model B to test, so right away, how about we delve in!

Brad Chacos

The Raspberry Pi 3 alongside a first-gen Moto X with a 4.7-inch show, for size correlation.

Quicker, better, harder, more grounded

The interest of the Raspberry Pi has constantly laid in what you do with it as opposed to crude tech specs, yet the equipment gives you a chance to make shockingly commonsense Raspberry Pi ventures and madly innovative developments alike. Before we jump into the progressions and execution, here's a speedy spec breakdown:

SoC: Broadcom BCM2837 64-bit framework on-chip with four ARM Cortex-A53 CPU centers timed 1.2GHz

CPU: 4X ARM Cortex-A53, 1.2GHz

GPU: Broadcom VideoCore IV

Slam: 1GB LPDDR2 (900MHz)

Organizing: 10/100 ethernet, 2.4GHz 802.11n remote

Bluetooth: Bluetooth 4.1 Classic, Bluetooth Low Energy

Capacity: microSD

GPIO: 40-stick header, populated

Ports: HDMI, 3.5mm simple sound video jack, 4X USB 2.0, ethernet, Camera Serial Interface (CSI), Display Serial Interface (DSI)

The card-sized Raspberry Pi 3's freshly discovered power lies in a trio of redesigns: another framework on-chip (SoC) with more strong design and processing abilities, installed 2.4GHz 802.11n Wi-Fi, and locally available Bluetooth 4.1/Low Energy bolster.

The new components appear to be immaterial on paper, yet they indicate a genuine convenience help in this present reality—particularly the installed remote capacities, which out and out work out of the case with the default/prescribed Raspbian working framework. Building up a Raspberry Pi-particular OS to work exclusively with Raspberry Pi equipment pays profits in convenience, it appears to be, particularly since standard Linux establishments are infamous for finicky remote availability. The simple actuality that coordinated Wi-Fi exists is an enormous stride up from past Raspberry Pi models, which required you either to horse up money for a Wi-Fi connector or hardwire your board by means of an ethernet association.

Brad Chacos

Clockwise from upper left: The Raspberry Pi, Raspberry Pi 2, and Raspberry Pi 3.

That is not by any means the only admission to comfort presented in the Raspberry Pi 3. One of the greatest migraines with the first Raspberry Pi was just associating all that you expected to it, as the underlying variant highlighted just a couple of USB 2.0 data sources. Interfacing the nuts and bolts—a USB console, mouse, and Wi-Fi connector—required a USB center, not notwithstanding specifying outer capacity drives or whatever other rigging you'd get a kick out of the chance to associate with the board. The Raspberry Pi 2 cured that migraine by multiplying the quantity of USB ports to four. The Raspberry Pi 3 runs above and beyond with local Bluetooth similarity, which proves to be useful for associating remote peripherals (observe, people who utilize the Raspberry Pi as a modest media gushing box) or devices and sensors for more propelled producer ventures.

Including the remote capacities didn't expand the Raspberry Pi's general impression, either. The new remote radio is small to the point that "its markings must be legitimately observed through a magnifying instrument or amplifying glass," the Raspberry Pi Foundation brags.

The Raspberry Pi 3's new SoC likewise gives it a major leg-up in execution over the Raspberry Pi 2, which itself destroyed the single-center unique Raspberry Pi. The Raspberry Pis 2 and 3 both shake quad-center processors, however the most recent release highlights a quartet of Cortex-A53 CPU centers timed at 1.2GHz, contrasted with the Raspberry Pi 2's 900MHz ARM Cortex-A7 centers. As such, the Raspberry Pi 3 has more proficient centers running at higher clock speeds. Both pack a Broadcom VideoCore IV illustrations processor, however the speed's been knock from 250MHz to 400MHz in the Raspberry Pi 3.

Chapter 2

The Raspbian working framework's default home screen.

Exhausting numbers aside, the SoC's specialized overhauls convey one serious execution and ease of use redesign. The Pi's fit for 1080p video playback at 60 outlines for each second now, up from 30fps earlier—however the prepared in Epiphany program gags on 60 fps YouTube recordings. Neighborhood recordings and also YouTube recordings viewed by means of the Iceweasel program (introduced independently) ran smooth as silk, in any case.

More vital is exactly how much the Raspberry Pi 3 neglects to advise you that you're utilizing a $35 PC. Past forms experienced irritating delays and slack when performing even fundamental errands like checking Gmail or overseeing records with LibreOffice, yet those cerebral pains are to a great extent gone in the Raspberry Pi 3. You won't mistake it for a Windows desktop or even a Chromebook, yet when Raspberry Pi Foundation originator Eben Upton said "This 50–60 percent [performance improvement] has moved us over some kind of line, where it turns into an a great deal more tenable PC substitution," he wasn't lying. The Raspberry Pi 3 can deal with essential efficiency undertakings and web perusing.

In spite of the fact that the Raspberry Pi's ARM-based processors render it inconsistent with many significant benchmarks, we ran a modest bunch of tests to measure the generational change. To do as such, we stacked the Raspberry Pi 2 and Raspberry Pi 3 with the most recent Raspbian Jessie manufacture kept up on the Raspberry Pi site.

Initially, we tried both frameworks with the Sunspider 1.0.2 Javascript benchmark in Raspbian's default Epiphany program. The outcomes (which you can snap to broaden) demonstrate what number of milliseconds it took to finish the benchmark, so lower results are better. Basically, the Raspberry Pi 3 overwhelms its forerunner in immaculate execution.

Similar remains constant for Google's Octane 2.0 test, which we benchmarked utilizing the Iceweasel program. Higher scores are better. The Raspberry Pi 3 practically pairs the Raspberry Pi 2's outcomes.

We additionally measured the frameworks' processing execution straightforwardly utilizing the long-running sysbench apparatus. We arranged the test to ascertain each prime number up to 20,000 utilizing both a solitary center, to decide the Raspberry Pi 3's single-string execution pick up...

... and in addition on every one of the four of every framework's centers. The outcomes demonstrate how long it took for every machine to play out the operation, so lower results are better. As should be obvious, the Raspberry Pi 3 cleaned the floor with its rival once more, completing estimations minutes in front of the Pi 2. Zoom!

Furthermore, recollect: The Raspberry Pi 2 conveyed four to five circumstances more execution than the first Raspberry Pi, so on the off chance that you redesign from the first model to the Raspberry Pi 3, get ready to be overwhelmed by its speed.

The entire Pi

It's noteworthy how (generally) intense the $35 Raspberry Pi 3 can be, however the board won't work without anyone else's input. You'll have to associate it to a screen or TV by means of HDMI; interface it to control through a 5-volt miniaturized scale USB line fit for drawing 2.5 amps from the divider (I utilized a Kindle Fire charger; my Moto X's charger wasn't adequate); and associate yourself by means of a USB or Bluetooth console and mouse, however you'll have to set it up utilizing USB peripherals before you can initiate Bluetooth matching. Snatching a case or if nothing else a container to house the Pi is a swell thought as well, in light of the fact that the board is completely uncovered in its default state.

Brad Chacos

The Raspberry Pi 3 needs a considerable measure of additional items to work. On the in addition to side, utilizing Bluetooth peripherals can free up your USB ports in the event that you require them.

You'll additionally need to bring your own working framework and capacity on a microSD card. (There's a decent possibility you'll have to microSD card connector to space the card into a customary PC and snatch that working framework, as well.) There is a wide universe of Raspberry Pi working frameworks accessible, from more broad Linux distros to laser-centered OSes worked for a particular reason, similar to Windows 10 IoT, OpenElec for media gushing, or a Raspbian work for Pi-controlled climate stations.

We tried the Raspberry Pi 3 with Raspbian, the Raspberry Pi Foundation's authoritatively bolstered working framework. The Foundation's Noobs installer instrument and setup manage makes getting your Raspberry Pi up and running moderately simple peasy, regardless of the possibility that OS establishments aren't your some tea.

Raspbian's a genuinely stripped-down working framework that drives home the Foundation's unique objective for the Raspberry Pi—to make a moderate PC that kids can use to learn software engineering.

A portion of the programming heated into Raspbian.

Past essential OS devices like picture viewers, the Epiphany program, and the LibreOffice efficiency suite, Rapbian's stuffed with improvement programming. You'll discover adaptations of Wolfram Mathematica, Python program creation devices, and Java coordinated improvement situations, alongside more straightforwardly engaging instructive programming like Scratch, a liveliness coding IDE for children, and Sonic Pi, "an open-source programming environment, intended for making new sounds with code in a live coding environment." There's additionally Minecraft Pi, a rendition of that blockbuster diversion that obliges you to utilize Python programming situations and ping the Minecraft Python API (in addition to other things) to play it.

Raspbian likewise houses a focal "Pi Store" with several extra instruments, or you can simply appreciate the code-driven concentration and snatch new programming through a Terminal window. (Perused: the charge line.) Raspbian offers all that you require in a fundamental working framework.

Primary concern

Brad Chacos

Furthermore, that is urgent, on the grounds that the Raspberry Pi 3's execution is at last sufficient to permit it to work as a fundamental PC, as opposed to being confined to wild creator activities or more functional reason driven particular employments. The Raspberry Pi 3 can in any case play out those particular undertakings, obviously—and in excess of anyone's imagination!—however now it can accomplish more. I'm likely going to set up my little girl with one for her schoolwork, which is something I'd never have considered with the past Raspberry Pi models.

Additionally perusing: Mini-PC intrusion: These drastically modest PCs fit in the palm of your hand

On paper, the Raspberry Pi 3 is only a more competent adaptation of its ancestors, however it's far beyond that as a general rule. While the Raspberry Pi 2 cured the first model's pokey execution and unimportant port determination, the Raspberry Pi 3's additional oomph and new remote abilities push it over a urgent ease of use protuberance. The availability bothers are no more. The moderate and stammering center experience feels smooth—or possibly sufficiently smooth—at this point. You no longer need to battle with the Raspberry Pi just to utilize it.

What's more, the Raspberry Pi 3 figures out how to accomplish all that in spite of adhering to the same $35 value point. On the off chance that you've ever had any enthusiasm for grabbing a Raspberry Pi to tinker with, or basically need an extremely inexpensive profitability PC, HTPC, or record server, the Raspberry Pi 3 comes profoundly prescribed. It's delectable.

Raspberry Pi

"RPi" diverts here. For different uses, see RPI.

Raspberry Pi 3 Model B (most recent adaptation)

Raspberry Pi 3 Model B

The Raspberry Pi is a progression of charge card estimated single-board PCs created in the United Kingdom by the Raspberry Pi Foundation to advance the educating of fundamental software engineering in schools and in creating countries.[3][4][5] The first model got to be distinctly significantly more prevalent than expected, offering outside of its objective market for utilizations, for example, mechanical technology. Extras including consoles, mice and cases are excluded with the Raspberry Pi. A few embellishments however have been incorporated into a few official and informal packs.

In February 2016, the Raspberry Pi Foundation declared that they had sold eight million gadgets (for all models joined), making it the top of the line UK PC, in front of the Amstrad PCW. Deals achieved ten million in September 2016.

Substance

Chapter 3

Review

A few eras of Raspberry Pis have been discharged. The original (Raspberry Pi 1 Model B) was discharged in February 2012. It was trailed by a less complex and reasonable Model A. In 2014, the establishment discharged a board with an enhanced outline in Raspberry Pi 1 Model B+. The model laid the current "mainline" shape calculate. Enhanced A+ and B+ models were discharged a year later. A chop down "figure module" was discharged in April 2014, and a Raspberry Pi Zero with littler size and restricted information/yield (I/O) and broadly useful info/yield (GPIO) capacities was discharged in November 2015 for US$5. The Raspberry Pi 2 which included more RAM was discharged in February 2015. Raspberry Pi 3 Model B discharged in February 2016 is packaged with on-board WiFi and Bluetooth. As of December 2016, Raspberry Pi 3 Model B is the most up to date mainline Raspberry Pi. These sheets are valued between US$5–35.

All models highlight a Broadcom framework on a chip (SoC), which incorporates an ARM perfect focal preparing unit (CPU) and an on chip representation handling unit (GPU, a VideoCore IV). CPU speed ranges from 700 MHz to 1.2 GHz for the Pi 3 and on board memory extend from 256 MB to 1 GB RAM. Secure Digital (SD) cards are utilized to store the working framework and program memory in either the SDHC or MicroSDHC sizes. Most sheets have somewhere around one and four USB spaces, HDMI and composite video yield, and a 3.5 mm telephone jack for sound. Bring down level yield is given by various GPIO pins which bolster regular conventions like I^2C. The B-models have a 8P8C Ethernet port and the Pi 3 has on board Wi-Fi 802.11n and Bluetooth.

The Foundation gives Raspbian, a Debian-based Linux conveyance for download, and additionally outsider Ubuntu, Windows 10 IOT Core, RISC OS, and specific media focus disseminations. It advances Python and Scratch as the fundamental programming dialect, with support for some different dialects. The default firmware is shut source, while an informal open source is accessible.

Equipment

The Raspberry Pi equipment has developed through a few forms that element varieties in memory limit and fringe gadget bolster.

This square chart delineates Models A, B, A+, and B+. Show An, A+, and the Pi Zero do not have the Ethernet and USB center parts. The Ethernet connector is inside associated with an extra USB port. In Model An, A+, and the PI Zero, the USB port is associated straightforwardly to the framework on a chip (SoC). On the Pi 1 Model B+ and later models the USB/Ethernet chip contains a five-point USB center, of which four ports are accessible, while the Pi 1 Model B just gives two. On the Pi Zero, the USB port is additionally associated straightforwardly to the SoC, yet it utilizes a smaller scale USB (OTG) port.

Processor

The Raspberry Pi 2 utilizes a 32-bit 900 MHz quad-center ARM Cortex-A7 processor.

The Broadcom BCM2835 SoC utilized as a part of the original Raspberry Pi is fairly proportional to the chip utilized as a part of original cell phones (its CPU is a more established ARMv6 design), which incorporates a 700 MHz ARM1176JZF-S processor, VideoCore IV representation preparing unit (GPU), and RAM. It has a level 1 (L1) reserve of 16 KB and a level 2 (L2) store of 128 KB. The level 2 store is utilized essentially by the GPU. The SoC is stacked underneath the RAM chip, so just its edge is unmistakable.

The Raspberry Pi 2 utilizes a Broadcom BCM2836 SoC with a 900 MHz 32-bit quad-center ARM Cortex-A7 processor (as do numerous current cell phones), with 256 KB shared L2 store.

The Raspberry Pi 3 utilizes a Broadcom BCM2837 SoC with a 1.2 GHz 64-bit quad-center ARM Cortex-A53 processor, with 512 KB shared L2 reserve.

Execution

While working at 700 MHz as a matter of course, the original Raspberry Pi gave a certifiable execution generally comparable to 0.041 GFLOPS. On the CPU level the execution is like a 300 MHz Pentium II of 1997–99. The GPU gives 1 Gpixel/s or 1.5 Gtexel/s of illustrations preparing or 24 GFLOPS of broadly useful processing execution. The graphical capacity of the Raspberry Pi are generally proportionate to the execution of the Xbox of 2001.

The LINPACK single hub register benchmark brings about a mean single exactness execution of 0.065 GFLOPS and a mean twofold accuracy execution of 0.041 GFLOPS for one Raspberry Pi Model-B board. A bunch of 64 Raspberry Pi Model B PCs, named "Iridis-pi", accomplished a LINPACK HPL suite consequence of 1.14 GFLOPS (n=10240) at 216 watts for c. US$4000.

Raspberry Pi 2 incorporates a quad-center Cortex-A7 CPU running at 900 MHz and 1 GB RAM. It is depicted as 4–6 circumstances more effective than its ancestor. The GPU is indistinguishable to the first. In parallelized benchmarks, the Raspberry Pi 2 could be up to 14 times speedier than a Raspberry Pi 1 Model B+.

The Raspberry Pi 3, with a quad-center Cortex-A53 processor, is portrayed as 10 times the execution of a Raspberry Pi 1. This was recommended to be very needy upon assignment threading and guideline set utilize. Benchmarks demonstrated the Raspberry Pi 3 to be around 80% speedier than the Raspberry Pi 2 in parallelized assignments.

Chapter 4

Overclocking

The original Raspberry Pi chip worked at 700 MHz as a matter of course, and did not get to be distinctly sufficiently hot to require a warmth sink or extraordinary cooling unless the chip was overclocked. The Raspberry Pi 2 keeps running at 900 MHz as a matter of course; it likewise does not get to be distinctly sufficiently hot to require a heatsink or uncommon cooling, despite the fact that overclocking may warm up the SoC more than expected.

Most Raspberry Pi chips could be overclocked to 800 MHz, and some to 1000 MHz. There are reports the Raspberry Pi 2 can be also overclocked, in outrageous cases, even to 1500 MHz (disposing of all wellbeing highlights and over-voltage impediments). In the Raspbian Linux distro the overclocking alternatives on boot should be possible by a product charge running "sudo raspi-config" without voiding the guarantee. In those cases the Pi consequently close the overclocking down if the chip comes to 85 °C (185 °F), however it is conceivable to abrogate programmed over-voltage and overclocking settings (voiding the guarantee); a fittingly estimated heatsink is expected to shield the chip from genuine overheating.

More up to date forms of the firmware contain the alternative to pick between five overclock ("turbo") presets that when utilized, endeavor to boost the execution of the SoC without impeding the lifetime of the load up. This is finished by observing the center temperature of the chip, the CPU stack, and progressively changing clock speeds and the center voltage. At the point when the request is low on the CPU or it is running excessively hot the execution is throttled, yet in the event that the CPU has much to do and the chip's temperature is satisfactory, execution is briefly expanded with clock rates of up to 1 GHz contingent upon the individual load up and on which of the turbo settings is utilized.

The seven overclock presets are:

- none; 700 MHz ARM, 250 MHz center, 400 MHz SDRAM, 0 overvolt,

- modest; 800 MHz ARM, 250 MHz center, 400 MHz SDRAM, 0 overvolt,

- medium; 900 MHz ARM, 250 MHz center, 450 MHz SDRAM, 2 overvolt,

- high; 950 MHz ARM, 250 MHz center, 450 MHz SDRAM, 6 overvolt,

- turbo; 1000 MHz ARM, 500 MHz center, 600 MHz SDRAM, 6 overvolt,

- Pi2; 1000 MHz ARM, 500 MHz center, 500 MHz SDRAM, 2 overvolt,

- Pi3; 1100 MHz ARM, 550 MHz center, 500 MHz SDRAM, 6 overvolt. In framework data CPU speed will show up as 1200 MHz. At the point when out of gear speed brings down to 600 MHz.

In the most noteworthy (turbo) preset the SDRAM clock was initially 500 MHz, yet this was later changed to 600 MHz since 500 MHz some of the time causes SD card defilement. At the same time in high mode the center clock speed was brought from 450 down to 250 MHz, and in medium mode from 333 to 250 MHz.

The Raspberry Pi Zero keeps running at 1 GHz.

Smash

On the more established beta Model B loads up, 128 MB was assigned of course to the GPU, leaving 128 MB for the CPU. On the initial 256 MB discharge Model B (and Model A), three unique parts were conceivable. The default split was 192 MB (RAM for CPU), which ought to be adequate for standalone 1080p video disentangling, or for basic 3D, yet presumably not for both together. 224 MB was for Linux just, with just a 1080p framebuffer, and was probably going to come up short for any video or 3D. 128 MB was for substantial 3D, perhaps at the same time with video disentangling (e.g. XBMC). Similarly the Nokia 701 utilizations 128 MB for the Broadcom VideoCore IV. For the new Model B with 512 MB RAM at first there were new standard memory split documents discharged(arm256_start.elf, arm384_start.elf, arm496_start.elf) for 256 MB, 384 MB and 496 MB CPU RAM (and 256 MB, 128 MB and 16 MB video RAM). In any case, a week or so later the RPF discharged another rendition of start.elf that could read another section in config.txt (gpu_mem=xx) and could progressively appoint a measure of RAM (from 16 to 256 MB in 8 MB ventures) to the GPU, so the more established technique for memory parts got to be distinctly out of date, and a solitary start.elf worked the same for 256 and 512 MB Raspberry Pis.

The Raspberry Pi 2 and the Raspberry Pi 3 have 1 GB of RAM. The Raspberry Pi Zero has 512 MB of RAM.

Organizing

The Model An, A+ and Pi Zero have no Ethernet hardware and are normally associated with a system utilizing an outside client provided USB Ethernet or Wi-Fi connector. On the Model B and B+ the Ethernet port is given by an implicit USB Ethernet connector utilizing the SMSC LAN9514 chip. The Raspberry Pi 3 is furnished with 2.4 GHz WiFi 802.11n (150 Mbit/s) and Bluetooth 4.1 (24 Mbit/s) notwithstanding the 10/100 Ethernet port.

Peripherals

The present Model B sheets join four USB ports for interfacing peripherals.

The Raspberry Pi might be worked with any nonexclusive USB PC console and mouse.

Video

The early Raspberry Pi 1 Model A, with a HDMI port and a standard RCA composite video port for more seasoned presentations.

The video controller can discharge standard current TV resolutions, for example, HD and Full HD, and higher or bring down screen resolutions and more seasoned standard CRT TV resolutions. As dispatched (i.e., without custom overclocking) it can emanate these: 640×350 EGA; 640×480 VGA; 800×600 SVGA; 1024×768 XGA; 1280×720 720p HDTV; 1280×768 WXGA variation; 1280×800 WXGA variation; 1280×1024 SXGA; 1366×768 WXGA variation; 1400×1050 SXGA+; 1600×1200 UXGA; 1680×1050 WXGA+; 1920×1080 1080p HDTV; 1920×1200 WUXGA.

Higher resolutions, for example, up to 2048×1152, may work or even 3840×2160 at 15 Hz (too low a framerate for persuading video). Note likewise that permitting the most noteworthy resolutions does not suggest that the GPU can interpret video positions at those; indeed, the Pis are known to not work dependably for H.265 (at those high determination, at any rate), regularly utilized for high resolutions (most arrangements, generally utilized, up to full HD, do work).

In spite of the fact that the Raspberry Pi 3 does not have H.265 unraveling equipment, the CPU, more intense than its forerunners, is possibly ready to translate H.265-encoded recordings in programming. The Open Source Media Center (OSMC) extend said in February 2016:

The new BCM2837 in light of 64-bit ARMv8 engineering is in reverse good with the Raspberry Pi 2 and in addition the first. While the new CPU is 64-bit, the Pi holds the first VideoCore IV GPU which has a 32-bit outline. It will be a couple of months before work is done to build up 64-bit pointer interfacing from the portion and userland on the ARM to the 32-bit GPU. In that capacity, until further notice, we will offer a solitary Raspberry Pi picture for Raspberry Pi 2 and the new Raspberry Pi 3. Just when 64-bit support is prepared, and gainful to OSMC clients, will we offer a different picture. The new quad center CPU will bring smoother GUI execution. There have additionally been late upgrades to H265 translating. While not equipment quickened on the Raspberry Pi, the new CPU will empower more H265 substance to be played back on the Raspberry Pi than some time recently.

— Raspberry Pi 3 declared with OSMC bolster

The Pi 3's GPU has higher clock frequencies – 300 MHz and 400 MHz for various parts – than past variants' 250 MHz.

The Raspberry Pis can likewise produce 576i and 480i composite video signals, as utilized on old-style (CRT) TV screens through standard connectors – either RCA or 3.5 mm telephone connector relying upon models. The TV flag guidelines bolstered are PAL-BGHID, PAL-M, PAL-N, NTSC and NTSC-J.

Ongoing clock

The Raspberry Pi does not have an implicit ongoing clock, and does not "know" the season of day. As a workaround, a program running on the Raspberry Pi can get the time from a system time server or client contribution at boot time, in this manner knowing the time while fueled on.

A constant equipment clock with battery reinforcement, for example, the DS1307, which is completely twofold coded, might be included (regularly by means of the I^2C interface).

Connectors

Pi Zero

-

Area of connectors and fundamental ICs
Model An/A+

-

Area of connectors and fundamental ICs
on Raspberry Pi 1 Model A

-

Area of connectors and fundamental ICs
on Raspberry Pi 1 Model A+ amendment
1.1 Model B/B+

-

Area of connectors and fundamental ICs on Raspberry Pi 1 Model B amendment 1.2

-

Area of connectors and fundamental ICs on Raspberry Pi 1 Model B+ amendment 1.2 and Raspberry Pi 2

-

Area of connectors and fundamental ICs on Raspberry Pi 3

Broadly useful info yield (GPIO) connector

Raspberry Pi 1 Models A+ and B+, Pi 2 Model B, Pi 3 Model B and Pi Zero GPIO J8 have a 40-stick pinout. Models An and B have just the initial 26 pins.

GPIO# 2nd func. Pin#   Pin# 2nd func. GPIO#

+3.3 V 1 2 +5 V

2 SDA1 (I^2C) 3 4 +5 V

3 SCL1 (I^2C) 5 6 GND

4 GCLK 7 8 TXD0 (UART) 14

GND 9 10 RXD0 (UART) 15

17 GEN0 11 12 GEN1 18

27 GEN2 13 14 GND

22 GEN3 15 16 GEN4 23

+3.3 V 17 18 GEN5 24

10 MOSI (SPI) 19 20 GND

9 MISO (SPI) 21 22 GEN6 25

11 SCLK (SPI) 23 24 CE0_N (SPI) 8

GND 25 26 CE1_N (SPI) 7

(Pi 1 Models An and B stop here)

EEPROM ID_SD 27 28 ID_SC EEPROM

5 N/A 29 30 GND

6 N/A 31 32 12

13 N/A 33 34 GND

19 N/A 35 36 N/A 16

26 N/A 37 38 Digital IN 20

GND 39 40 Digital OUT 21

Demonstrate B rev. 2 likewise has a cushion (called P5 on the board and P6 on the schematics) of 8 pins offering access to an extra 4 GPIO associations.

Function 2nd func. Pin# Pin# 2nd func. Function

N/A +5 V 1 2 +3.3 V N/A

GPIO28 GPIO_GEN7 3   4 GPIO_GEN8 GPIO29

GPIO30 GPIO_GEN9 5 6 GPIO_GEN10 GPIO31

N/A GND 7 8 GND N/A

Models An and B give GPIO access to the ACT status LED utilizing GPIO 16. Models A+ and B+ give GPIO access to the ACT status LED utilizing GPIO 47, and the power status LED utilizing GPIO 35.

Embellishments

• Camera – On 14 May 2013, the establishment and the merchants RS Components and Premier Farnell/Element 14 propelled the Raspberry Pi camera board with a firmware redesign to oblige it. The camera board is sent with an adaptable level link that attachments into the CSI connector situated between the Ethernet and HDMI ports. In Raspbian, one empowers the framework to utilize the camera board by the introducing or moving up to the most recent adaptation of the working framework (OS) and afterward running Raspi-config and selecting the camera choice. The cost of the camera module is €20 in Europe (9 September 2013). It can deliver 1080p, 720p and 640x480p video. The measurements are 25 mm × 20 mm × 9 mm. In May 2016, v2 of the camera turned out, and is a 8 megapixel camera.

• Gertboard – A Raspberry Pi Foundation authorized gadget, intended for instructive purposes, that grows the Raspberry Pi's GPIO pins to permit interface with and control of LEDs, switches, simple signs, sensors and different gadgets. It likewise incorporates a discretionary Arduino good controller to interface with the Pi.

• Infrared Camera – In October 2013, the establishment reported that they would start delivering a camera module without an infrared channel, called the Pi NoIR.

• HAT (Hardware Attached on Top) development sheets – Together with the Model B+, propelled by the Arduino shield sheets, the interface for HAT sheets was contrived by the Raspberry Pi Foundation. Every HAT board conveys a little EEPROM (ordinarily a CAT24C32WI-GT3) containing the significant subtle elements of the board, so that the Raspberry Pi's OS is educated of the HAT, and the specialized points of interest of it, important to the OS utilizing the HAT. Mechanical points of interest of a HAT board, that utilization the four mounting openings in their rectangular arrangement, are accessible on the web.

Programming

Working frameworks

Different working frameworks can be introduced on the Raspberry Pi through SD cards; most utilize a MicroSD space situated on the base of the board.

The Raspberry Pi essentially utilizes Raspbian, a Debian-based Linux working framework. Other outsider working frameworks accessible by means of the official site incorporate Ubuntu MATE, Snappy Ubuntu Core, Windows 10 IoT Core, RISC OS and specific conveyances for the Kodi media focus and classroom administration.

Numerous other working frameworks can likewise keep running on the Raspberry Pi.

Other working frameworks (not Linux-based)

• RISC OS Pi (an extraordinary chop down variant RISC OS Pico, for 16 MB cards and bigger for all models of Pi 1 and 2, has additionally been made accessible.)

• FreeBSD

• NetBSD

• Plan 9 from Bell Labs and Inferno (in beta)

- Windows 10 IoT Core – a no-cost release of Windows 10 offered by Microsoft that runs locally on the Raspberry Pi 2.

- xv6 – is a current reimplementation of Sixth Edition Unix OS for showing purposes; it is ported to Raspberry Pi from MIT xv6; this xv6 port can boot from NOOBS.

- Haiku – is an opensource BeOS clone that has can be ordered for the Raspberry Pi and a few other ARM sheets. Chip away at Pi 1 started in 2011, yet just the Pi 2 will be bolstered.

- HelenOS – a convenient microkernel-based multiserver working framework; has essential Raspberry Pi bolster since form 0.6.0

- Genode OS Framework – bolsters the Raspberry Pi stage with the base-hw piece since discharge 13.05 Other working frameworks (Linux-based)

- Xbian – utilizing the Kodi (once in the past XBMC) open source advanced media focus

- openSUSE

- Raspberry Pi Fedora Remix

- Pidora, another Fedora Remix upgraded for the Raspberry Pi

- Gentoo Linux

- Diet Pi, incorporates an assorted scope of servers for media, VPN, Minecraft and numerous others

- CentOS for Raspberry Pi 2 and later

• RedSleeve (a RHEL port) for Raspberry Pi 1

• Slackware ARM – form 13.37 and later keeps running on the Raspberry Pi without alteration. The 128–496 MB of accessible memory on the Raspberry Pi is at any rate double the base necessity of 64 MB expected to run Slackware Linux on an ARM or i386 framework. (While the dominant part of Linux frameworks boot into a graphical UI, Slackware's default client environment is the printed shell/order line interface.) The Fluxbox window chief running under the X Window System requires an extra 48 MB of RAM.

• Moebius – is a light ARM HF conveyance in view of Debian. It utilizes Raspbian vault, however it fits in a 128 MB SD card. It has just insignificant administrations and its memory utilize is upgraded to be little.

- OpenWrt – is essentially utilized on implanted gadgets to course arrange movement.

- Kali Linux – is a Debian-determined distro intended for computerized legal sciences and entrance testing.

- Pardus ARM – is a Debian-based working framework which is the light form of the Pardus (working framework).

- Instant WebKiosk – is a working framework for computerized signage purposes (web and media sees).

- Ark OS – is intended for site and email self-facilitating.

- ROKOS – is a Raspbian-based working framework with incorporated customers for the Bitcoin and OKCash cryptocurrencies.

- MinePeon – is a devoted working framework for mining cryptocurrency.

- Kano OS

- Nard SDK – is a product advancement pack (SDK) for mechanical inserted frameworks.

- Sailfish OS with Raspberry Pi 2 (because of utilization ARM Cortex-A7 CPU; Raspberry Pi 1 utilizes diverse ARMv6 design and Sailfish requires ARMv7.)

- Tiny Core Linux – a negligible Linux working framework concentrated on giving a base framework utilizing BusyBox and FLTK. Intended to run basically in RAM.

- IPFire – is a committed firewall/switch conveyance for the security of a SOHO LAN; runs just on a Raspberry Pi 1; porting to the Raspberry Pi 2 is not made arrangements for now.

• Alpine Linux – is a Linux dispersion in light of musl and BusyBox, basically intended for "power clients who acknowledge security, straightforwardness and asset productivity".

• Void Linux – a moving discharge Linux conveyance which was composed and executed starting with no outside help, gives pictures in light of musl or glibc.

• Tingbot OS – in view of Raspbian, principally intended for use with the Tingbot addon and running Tide applications.

• WTware for Raspberry Pi – is a free working framework for making Windows thin customer from Pi 2 and Pi 3.

• Fedora 25 – underpins Pi 2 and later (Pi 1 is upheld by some informal subordinates, e.g. recorded here.).

- Media focus working frameworks:

o OSMC

o OpenELEC

o LibreELEC

o Xbian

o Rasplex

- Audio working frameworks :

o Volumio

o Pimusicbox

o Runeaudio

o moOdeaudio

• Retrogaming working frameworks:

o Retropie

o Recalbox

o Happi Game Center

o Lakka

o ChameleonPi

o Piplay

Driver APIs

See additionally: VideoCore § Linux bolster

Plan of the actualized APIs: OpenMAX, OpenGL ES and OpenVG

Raspberry Pi can utilize a VideoCore IV GPU by means of a paired blob, which is stacked into the GPU at boot time from the SD-card, and extra programming, that at first was shut source. This part of the driver code was later discharged. Be that as it may, a great part of the genuine driver work is done utilizing the shut source GPU code. Application programming use calls to shut source run-time libraries (OpenMax, OpenGL ES or OpenVG) which thus calls an open source driver inside the Linux bit, which then calls the shut source VideoCore IV GPU driver code. The API of the part driver is particular for these shut libraries. Video applications utilize OpenMAX, 3D applications utilize OpenGL ES and 2D applications utilize OpenVG which both thus utilize EGL. OpenMAX and EGL utilize the open source piece driver thus.

Chapter 5

Firmware

The official firmware is an openly redistributable double blob, that is shut source. A negligible open source firmware is likewise accessible.

Outsider application programming

• AstroPrint – AstroPrint's Wireless 3D printing programming can be keep running on the Pi 2.

• Mathematica and the Wolfram Language – Since 21 November 2013, Raspbian incorporates a full establishment of this exclusive programming for nothing. Starting 24 August 2015, the form is Mathematica 10.2. Projects can be run either from a summon line interface or from a Notebook interface. There are Wolfram Language capacities for getting to associated gadgets. There is additionally a Wolfram Language desktop improvement unit permitting advancement for Raspberry Pi in Mathematica from desktop machines.

• Minecraft – Released 11 February 2013, a form for the Raspberry Pi, in which you can alter the diversion world with code, the main authority rendition of the amusement in which you can do as such.

• UserGate Web Filter – On 20 September 2013, Florida-based security merchant Entensys declared porting UserGate Web Filter to Raspberry Pi stage.

Programming improvement apparatuses

• Arduino IDE - for programming an arduino.

• AlgoID – for learning programming for children and novices.

• BlueJ – for instructing Java to novices.

• Fawlty Language – a uninhibitedly usable IDL (programming dialect) clone for Pi 2.

• Greenfoot – Greenfoot shows *q*uestion introduction with Java. Make "on-screen characters" which live in "universes" to assemble recreations, reenactments, and other graphical projects.

• Julia – an intuitive and cross-stage programming dialect/environment, that keeps running on the Pi 1 and later. IDEs for Julia, for example, Juno, are accessible. See likewise Pi-particular vault JuliaBerry.

• Lazarus – a Free Pascal RAD IDE.

• LiveCode – instructive RAD IDE plummeted from HyperCard utilizing

English-like dialect to compose occasion handlers for WYSIWYG gadgets runnable on desktop, portable and Raspberry Pi stages.

• Ninja-IDE – a cross-stage incorporated improvement environment (IDE) for Python.

• Object Pascal – a protest situated variation (the one utilized as a part of Delphi IDE) of Niklaus Wirth's unique Pascal dialect.

• Processing – an IDE worked for the electronic expressions, new media craftsmanship, and visual outline groups with the motivation behind educating the essentials of PC programming in a visual setting.

• Scratch – a cross stage showing IDE utilizing visual obstructs that stack like Lego™ initially created by MIT's Life Long Kindergarten amass. The Pi rendition is vigorously enhanced for the restricted figure assets accessible and is actualized in the S*q*ueak Smalltalk framework.

- S*q*ueak Smalltalk – a full scale open Smalltalk.

- V-Play Game Engine – a cross-stage improvement system that backings versatile amusement and application advancement with the V-Play Game Engine, V-Play applications and V-Play modules.

- Xojo – a cross-stage, proficient RAD device that can make desktop, web and support applications for Pi 2.

- PowerBerry – a port of POWER-KI programming dialect on Windows 10 IoT – The PowerBerry Manager (PBM) permits the overseeing of the board and its dissemination contains demo and test Apps (GPIO, WEB, PCA9685).

Gathering and utilize

Innovation author Glyn Moody depicted the venture in May 2011 as a "potential BBC Micro 2.0", not by supplanting PC perfect machines but rather by supplementing them. In March 2012 Stephen Pritchard reverberated the BBC Micro successor feeling in ITPRO. Alex Hope, co-creator of the Next Gen report, is cheerful that the PC will draw in kids with the fervor of programming. Co-creator Ian Livingstone proposed that the BBC could be included in building support for the gadget, conceivably marking it as the BBC Nano. Chris Williams, writing in The Register sees the incorporation of programming dialects, for example, Kids Ruby, Scratch and BASIC as a "decent begin" to furnish kids with the aptitudes required later on – in spite of the fact that it stays to be perceived how compelling their utilization will be. The Center for Computing History firmly underpins the Raspberry Pi extend, feeling that it could "introduce another time". Before discharge, the board was showcased by ARM's CEO Warren East at an occasion in Cambridge laying out Google's thoughts to enhance UK science and innovation training.

Harry Fairhead, be that as it may, recommends that more accentuation ought to be put on enhancing the instructive programming accessible on existing equipment, utilizing devices, for example, Google App Inventor to return programming to schools, instead of including new equipment decisions. Simon Rockman, writing in a ZDNet blog, was of the assessment that teenagers will have "better things to do", in spite of what happened in the 1980s.

In October 2012, the Raspberry Pi won T3's Innovation of the Year honor, and futurist Mark Pesce refered to an (obtained) Raspberry Pi as the motivation for his encompassing gadget extend MooresCloud. In October 2012, the British Computer Society responded to the declaration of improved particulars by expressing, "it's unquestionably something we'll need to sink our teeth into."

In February 2015, an exchanged mode control supply chip, assigned U16, of the Raspberry Pi 2 Model B adaptation 1.1

(the at first discharged variant) was observed to be helpless against flashes of light, especially the light from xenon camera flashes and green and red laser pointers. In any case, other splendid lights, especially ones that are on ceaselessly, were found to have no impact. The side effect was the Raspberry Pi 2 suddenly rebooting or killing when these lights were flashed at the chip. At first, a few clients and analysts presumed that the electromagnetic heartbeat (EMP) from the xenon streak tube was bringing on the issue by meddling with the PC's advanced hardware, however this was discounted by tests where the light was either obstructed by a card or went for the opposite side of the Raspberry Pi 2, both of which did not bring about an issue. The issue was contracted down to the U16 chip by covering first the framework on a chip (principle processor) and afterward U16 with Blu-Tack (a hazy notice mounting compound). Light being the sole offender, rather than EMP, was further affirmed by the laser pointer tests, where it was likewise found that less dark covering was expected to shield against the laser pointers than to shield against the xenon flashes. The U16 chip is by all accounts exposed silicon without a plastic cover (i.e. a chip-scale bundle or wafer-level bundle), which would, if show, obstruct the light. Informal workarounds incorporate covering U16 with misty material, (for example, electrical tape enamel, blurb mounting compound, or even bunched up bread), putting the Raspberry Pi 2 for a situation, and abstaining from taking photographs of the top side of the board with a xenon streak. This issue was not got before the arrival of the Raspberry Pi 2 in light of the fact that while business electronic gadgets are routinely subjected to trial of powerlessness to radio impedance, it is not standard or normal practice to test their defenselessness to optical obstruction.

Group

The Raspberry Pi people group was depicted by Jamie Ayre of FLOSS programming organization AdaCore as a standout amongst the most energizing parts of the venture. Group blogger Russell Davis said that the group quality permits the Foundation to focus on documentation and educating. The people group built up a fanzine around the stage called The MagPi which in 2015, was given over to the Raspberry Pi Foundation by its volunteers to be proceeded in-house. A progression of group Raspberry Jam occasions have been held over the UK and around the globe.

Use in instruction

As of January 2012, enquiries about the load up in the United Kingdom have been gotten from schools in both the state and private segments, with around five circumstances as much enthusiasm from the last mentioned. It is sought that organizations will support buys after less advantaged schools. The CEO of Premier Farnell said that the administration of a nation in the Middle East has communicated enthusiasm for giving a board to each schoolgirl, so as to improve her work prospects.

In 2014, the Raspberry Pi Foundation employed some of its group individuals including ex-instructors and programming designers to dispatch an arrangement of free learning assets for its site. The assets are uninhibitedly authorized under Creative Commons, and commitments and joint efforts are empowered on social coding stage GitHub.

The Foundation additionally began an educator instructional class called Picademy with the point of helping instructors get ready for educating the new registering educational modules utilizing the Raspberry Pi as a part of the classroom. The proceeded with expert advancement course is sans given to educators and is controlled by the Foundation's instruction group.

Use in home robotization

There are various designers and applications that are utilizing the Raspberry Pi for home computerization. These software engineers are attempting to alter the Raspberry Pi into a cost moderate arrangement in vitality observing and control utilization. In view of the generally minimal effort of the Raspberry Pi, this has turned into a mainstream and efficient answer for the more costly business choices.

Use in business items

OTTO is an advanced camera made by Next Thing Co. It consolidates a Raspberry Pi Compute Module. It was effectively swarm financed in a May 2014 Kickstarter crusade.

Cut is an advanced media player which likewise utilizes a Compute Module as its heart. It was pack subsidized in an August 2014 Kickstarter crusade. The product running on Slice depends on Kodi.

Astro Pi

A venture was propelled in December 2014 at an occasion held by the UK Space Agency. The Astro Pi rivalry was formally opened in January and was opened to all essential and optional school matured youngsters who were occupants of the United Kingdom. Amid his main goal, British ESA Astronaut Tim Peake arrangements to send the PCs on board the International Space Station. He will then load up the triumphant code while in circle, gather the information produced and after that send this to Earth where it will be dispersed to the triumphant groups. The subjects of Spacecraft Sensors, Satellite Imaging, Space Measurements, Data Fusion and Space Radiation were concocted to invigorate innovative and logical considering.

The associations required in the Astro Pi rivalry incorporate the UK Space Agency, UKspace, Raspberry Pi, ESERO-UK and ESA.

HistoryThis segment contains installed records that might be better introduced utilizing composition. You can help by changing over the rundown or records to exposition, if fitting. Altering help is accessible. (February 2015) (Learn how and when to expel this layout message)

An early alpha-test board in operation utilizing distinctive format from later beta and generation sheets

In 2006, early ideas of the Raspberry Pi depended on the Atmel ATmega644 microcontroller. Its schematics and PCB design are freely accessible. Establishment trustee Eben Upton amassed a gathering of educators, scholastics and PC lovers to devise a PC to motivate youngsters. The PC is motivated by Acorn's BBC Micro of 1981. The Model A, Model B and Model B+ names are references to the first models of the British instructive BBC Micro PC, created by Acorn Computers. The principal ARM model form of the PC was mounted in a bundle an indistinguishable size from a USB memory stick. It had a USB port toward one side and a HDMI port on the other.

The Foundation's objective was to offer two adaptations, valued at US$25 and 35.

They began tolerating orders for the higher estimated Model B on 29 February 2012, the lower cost Model An on 4 February 2013. what's more, the even lower cost (US$20) A+ on 10 November 2014. On 26 November 2015, the least expensive Raspberry PI yet, the Raspberry PI Zero, was propelled at US$5 or £4.

Pre-dispatch

• July 2011: Trustee Eben Upton freely moved toward the RISC OS Open people group in July 2011 to enquire about help with a port. Adrian Lees at Broadcom has since chipped away at the port, with his work being refered to in a dialog in regards to the design drivers. This port is currently incorporated into NOOBS.

• August 2011 – 50 alpha sheets are fabricated. These sheets were practically indistinguishable to the arranged Model B, however they were physically bigger to oblige troubleshoot headers. Exhibitions of the board indicated it running the

LXDE desktop on Debian, Quake 3 at 1080p, and Full HD MPEG-4 video over HDMI.

• October 2011 – A rendition of RISC OS 5 was exhibited out in the open, and taking after a year of advancement the port was discharged for general utilization in November 2012.

• December 2011 – Twenty-five Model B Beta sheets were collected and tried from one hundred uninhabited PCBs. The part format of the Beta sheets was the same as on creation sheets. A solitary blunder was found in the board plan where a few sticks on the CPU were not held high; it was settled for the main generation run. The Beta sheets were exhibited booting Linux, playing a 1080p film trailer and the Rightware Samurai OpenGL ES benchmark.

• Early 2012 – During the principal week of the year, the initial 10 barricades were put available to be purchased on eBay. One was purchased secretly and gave to the exhibition hall at The Center for Computing History in Cambridge, England. The ten sheets (with an aggregate retail cost of £220) together raised over £16,000, with the last to be sold, serial number No. 01, raising £3,500. Ahead of time of the foreseen dispatch toward the end of February 2012, the Foundation's servers attempted to adapt to the heap set by watchers over and over reviving their programs.

Dispatch

• 19 February 2012 – The principal evidence of idea SD card picture that could be stacked onto a SD card to deliver a preparatory working framework is discharged. The picture depended on Debian 6.0 (Squeeze), with the LXDE desktop and the Midori program, in addition to different programming instruments. The picture additionally keeps running on QEMU permitting the Raspberry Pi to be copied on different stages.

• 29 February 2012 – Initial deals start 29 February 2012 at 06:00 UTC;. In the meantime, it was reported that the model An, initially to have had 128 MB of RAM, was to be moved up to 256 MB before discharge. The Foundation's site likewise reported: "Six years after the venture's commencement, we're about toward the end of our first keep running of advancement – in spite of the fact that it's simply the start of the Raspberry Pi story." The web-shops of the two authorized makers offering Raspberry Pi's inside the United Kingdom, Premier Farnell and RS Components, had their sites slowed down by substantial web movement quickly after the dispatch (RS Components quickly going down totally). Unverified reports proposed that there were more than two million articulations of intrigue or pre-orders. The official Raspberry Pi Twitter account reported that Premier Farnell sold out inside a couple of minutes of the underlying dispatch, while RS Components assumed control 100,000 pre arranges on the very beginning. Producers were accounted for in March 2012 to take a "solid number" of pre-requests.

• March 2012 – Shipping delays for the primary group were reported in March 2012, as the aftereffect of establishment of an erroneous Ethernet port, however the Foundation expected that assembling amounts of future bunches could be expanded with little trouble if require "We have guaranteed we can get them [the Ethernet connectors with magnetics] in huge numbers and Premier Farnell and RS Components [the two distributors] have been awesome at sourcing parts," Upton said. The principal group of 10,000 sheets was made in Taiwan and China.

• 8 March 2012 – Release Raspberry Pi Fedora Remix, the suggested Linux dispersion, created at Seneca College in Canada.

• March 2012 – The Debian port is started by Mike Thompson, previous CTO of Atomz. The exertion was to a great extent did by Thompson and Peter Green, a volunteer Debian designer, with some support from the Foundation, who tried the subsequent parallels that the two delivered amid the early stages (neither

Thompson nor Green had physical access to the equipment, as loads up were not generally available at the time because of interest). While the preparatory verification of idea picture conveyed by the Foundation before dispatch was likewise Debian-based, it contrasted from Thompson and Green's Raspbian exertion in two or three ways. The POC picture depended on then-stable Debian Squeeze, while Raspbian planned to track then-forthcoming Debian Wheezy bundles. Beside the overhauled bundles that would accompany the new discharge, Wheezy was additionally set to present the armhf engineering, which turned into the raison d'être for the Raspbian exertion. The Squeeze-based POC picture was constrained to the armel engineering, which was, at the season of Squeeze's discharge, the most recent endeavor by the Debian venture to have Debian keep running on the freshest ARM installed application double interface (EABI). The armhf engineering in Wheezy planned to make Debian keep running on the ARM VFP equipment drifting point unit, while armel was restricted to imitating gliding point operations in programming. since the Raspberry Pi incorporated a VFP, having the capacity to make utilization of the equipment unit would bring about execution picks up and diminished power use for coasting point operations. The armhf exertion in mainline Debian, in any case, was orthogonal to the work encompassing the Pi and just proposed to permit Debian to keep running on ARMv7 at any rate, which would mean the Pi, an ARMv6 gadget, would not profit. Therefore, Thompson and Green set out to assemble the 19,000 Debian bundles for the gadget utilizing a custom form group.

Post-dispatch

- 16 April 2012 – Reports show up from the principal purchasers who had gotten their Raspberry Pi.

- 20 April 2012 – The schematics for the Model An and Model B are discharged.

- 18 May 2012 – The Foundation provided details regarding its blog about a model camera module they had tried.

The model utilized a 14-megapixel module.

- 22 May 2012 – Over 20,000 units had been delivered.

- 16 July 2012 – It was reported that 4,000 units were being produced every day, permitting Raspberry Pis to be purchased in mass.

- 24 August 2012 – Hardware quickened video (H.264) encoding gets to be distinctly accessible after it got to be distinctly realized that the current permit likewise secured encoding. Once in the past it was suspected that encoding would be included with the arrival of the reported camera module. Notwithstanding, no steady programming exists for equipment H.264 encoding. In the meantime the Foundation discharged two extra codecs that can be purchased independently, MPEG-2 and Microsoft's VC-1. Likewise it was reported that the Pi will actualize CEC, empowering it to be controlled with the TV's remote control.

• July 2012 – Release of Raspbian.

• 5 September 2012 – The Foundation reported a moment amendment of the Raspberry Pi Model B. An amendment 2.0 board is reported, with various minor remedies and upgrades.

• 6 September 2012 – Announcement that in future the main part of Raspberry Pi units would be produced in the UK, at Sony's assembling office in Pencoed, Wales. The Foundation assessed that the plant would deliver 30,000 units for every month, and would make around 30 new employments.

• 15 October 2012 – It is reported that new Raspberry Pi Model Bs are to be fitted with 512 MB rather than 256 MB RAM.

• 24 October 2012 – The Foundation reports that "the greater part of the VideoCore driver code which keeps running on the ARM" had been discharged as free programming under a BSD-style permit, making it "the main ARM-based sight and sound SoC with completely useful, seller gave (instead of halfway, figured out) completely open-source drivers", despite the fact that this claim has not been all around acknowledged. On 28 February 2014, they likewise declared the arrival of full documentation for the VideoCore IV design center, and a total source arrival of the representation stack under a 3-provision BSD permit

• October 2012 – It was accounted for that a few clients of one of the two primary merchants had been sitting tight over six months for their requests. This was accounted for to be because of troubles in sourcing the CPU and traditionalist deals guaging by this wholesaler.

• 17 December 2012 – The Foundation, in a joint effort with IndieCity and Velocix, opens the Pi Store, as a "one-stop look for all your Raspberry Pi (programming) needs". Utilizing an application included as a part of Raspbian, clients can peruse through a few classifications and download what they need. Programming can likewise be transferred for balance and discharge.

• 3 June 2013 – 'New Out Of Box Software or NOOBS is presented. This makes the Raspberry Pi less demanding to use by disentangling the establishment of a working framework. Rather than utilizing particular programming to set up a SD card, a record is unfastened and the substance duplicated over to a FAT organized (4 GB or greater) SD card. That card can then be booted on the Raspberry Pi and a decision of six working frameworks is displayed for establishment on the card. The framework likewise contains a recuperation segment that takes into account the fast reclamation of the introduced OS, devices to alter the config.txt and an online catch and web program which coordinates to the Raspberry Pi Forums.

• October 2013 – The Foundation declares that the one millionth Pi had been produced in the United Kingdom.

• November 2013: they declare that the two millionth Pi delivered somewhere around 24 and 31 October.

• 28 February 2014 – upon the arrival of the second commemoration of the Raspberry Pi, Broadcom, together with the Raspberry PI establishment, reported the arrival of full documentation for the VideoCore IV design center, and an entire source arrival of the representation stack under a 3-condition BSD permit.

Raspberry Pi Compute Module

Raspberry Pi Model B

• 7 April 2014 – The official Raspberry Pi blog reported the Raspberry Pi Compute Module, a gadget in a 200-stick DDR2 SO-

DIMM-arranged memory module (however not at all perfect with such RAM), proposed for purchaser hardware originators to use as the center of their own items.

• June 2014 – The official Raspberry Pi blog said that the three millionth Pi dispatched toward the beginning of May 2014.

• 14 July 2014 – The official Raspberry Pi blog declared the Raspberry Pi Model B+, "the last advancement of the first Raspberry Pi. At an indistinguishable cost from the first Raspberry Pi display B, yet consolidating various little changes individuals have been requesting".

• 10 November 2014 – The official Raspberry Pi blog reported the Raspberry Pi Model A+. It is the littlest and least expensive (US$20) Raspberry Pi so far and has an indistinguishable processor and RAM from the model A. Like the An, it has no Ethernet port, and just a single USB port, however has alternate advancements of the B+, similar to lower control, miniaturized scale SD-card space, and 40-stick HAT good GPIO.

• 2 February 2015 – The official Raspberry Pi blog reported the Raspberry Pi 2. Resembling a Model B+, it has a 900 MHz quad-center ARMv7 Cortex-A7 CPU, double the memory (for a sum of 1 GB) and finish similarity with the first era of Raspberry Pis.

• 14 May 2015 – The cost of Model B+ was diminished from US$35 to 25, purportedly as a "reaction of the generation enhancements" from the Pi 2 improvement. Industry spectators have distrustfully noted, nonetheless, that the value drop had all the earmarks of being an immediate reaction to the C.H.I.P., a lower-evaluated contender.

• 26 November 2015 – The Raspberry Pi Foundation propelled the Raspberry Pi Zero, the littlest and least expensive individual from the Raspberry Pi family yet, at 65 mm × 30 mm, and US$5. The Zero is like the model A+ without camera and LCD connectors, while littler and utilizes less power. It was given away with the Raspberry PI magazine Magpi #40 that was appropriated in the UK and US that day – the MagPi was sold out at practically every retailer universally because of the freebie.

• 29 February 2016 – Raspberry Pi 3 with a BCM2837 1.2 GHz 64-bit quad processor in view of the ARMv8 Cortex A53, with inherent Wi-Fi BCM43438 802.11n 2.4 GHz and Bluetooth 4.1 Low Energy (BLE). Beginning with a 32-bit Raspbian variant, with a 64-bit form later to come if "there is esteem in moving to 64-bit mode". In a similar declaration it was said that another BCM2837 based Compute Module was relied upon to be presented a couple of months after the fact.

• 25 April 2016 – Raspberry Pi Camera v2.1 declared with 8 Mpixels, in typical and NoIR (can get IR) renditions. The camera utilizes the Sony IMX219 chip with a determination of 3280 × 2464. To make utilization of the new determination the product must be upgraded.

• 10 October 2016 – NEC Display Solutions reports that select models of business presentations to be discharged in mid 2017 will join a Raspberry Pi 3 Compute Module.

• 14 October 2016 – Raspberry Pi Foundation reports their collaboration with NEC Display Solutions. They expect that the Raspberry Pi 3 Compute Module will be accessible to the overall population before the end of 2016.

Conclusion

Thank you again for downloading this book!

I hope this book was able to help you to UNDERSTAND MORE ON Raspberry PI 3: The Ultimate Beginner's Guide

Finally, if you enjoyed this book, then I'd like to ask you for a favor, would you be kind enough to leave a review for this book on Amazon? It'd be greatly appreciated!

Thank you and good luck!

I truly do appreciate it!

Best Wishes,

Lee Maxwell

www.ingramcontent.com/pod-product-compliance
Lightning Source LLC
Chambersburg PA
CBHW060950050326
40689CB00012B/2619